WHAT THE
BIBLE
SAYS ABOUT
MANAGING
STRESS

What the Bible Says about Managing Stress
by Criswell Freeman

©2018 Smith Freeman Publishing

Bible verses were taken from the following translations:

Scripture quotations marked HCSB® are taken from the Holman Christian Standard Bible®, Copyright © 1999, 2000, 2002, 2003, 2009 by Holman Bible Publishers. Used by permission. HCSB® is a federally registered trademark of Holman Bible Publishers.

Scripture quotations marked KJV are from the King James Version. Public domain.

Scripture quotations marked MSG are taken from THE MESSAGE, copyright © 1993, 1994, 1995, 1996, 2000, 2001, 2002 by Eugene H. Peterson. Used by permission of NavPress. All rights reserved. Represented by Tyndale House Publishers, Inc.

Scripture quotations marked NASB are from the New American Standard Bible® (NASB), Copyright © 1960, 1962, 1963,1968, 1971, 1972, 1973, 1975, 1977, 1995 by the Lockman Foundation. Used by permission. www.Lockman.org.

Scripture quotations marked NCV are from the New Century Version®. Copyright by Thomas Nelson. Used by permission. All rights reserved.

Scripture quotations marked NIV are from The Holy Bible, New International Version® NIV® copyright © 1973, 1978, 1984, 2011 by Biblica, Inc. Used by permission. All rights reserved worldwide.

Scripture quotations marked NKJV are from the New King James Version®. Copyright © 1982 by Thomas Nelson. Used by permission. All rights reserved.

Scripture quotations marked NLT are from the Holy Bible, New Living Translation, copyright © 1996, 2004, 2015 by Tyndale House Foundation. Used by permission of Tyndale House Publishers, Inc., Carol Stream, Illinois 60188. All rights reserved.

Cover design by Kim Russell | Wahoo Designs

ISBN: 978-0-9997706-9-6

WHAT THE
BIBLE
SAYS ABOUT
MANAGING
STRESS

BY CRISWELL FREEMAN

CONTENTS

A MESSAGE TO READERS

Oliver Wendell Holmes Sr. observed, "Life is a great bundle of little things." And the same can be said for stress. Usually we are stressed by an assortment of things that start small but soon begin to add up. If we could simply focus on a single stressful event, we could probably tackle it. But life seldom works that way. Usually we have many items on our to-do lists, and each item seems to be crying out for immediate attention. So if we're not careful we find ourselves rushing from place to place, struggling to get everything done, feeling stressed out or burned out or both.

On the pages that follow, you'll be asked to think about ways that you and God, working together, can organize your life, prioritize your responsibilities, redirect your thoughts, and minimize your stressors. When you do these things, you'll receive the peace and the spiritual abundance that can, and should, be yours.

This text contains biblically based prescriptions for the inevitable challenges that accompany everyday life. As you consider your own circumstances, remember this: Whatever the size of your problems, God is bigger. Much bigger. He will instruct you, protect you, energize you, and heal you if you let Him.

So let Him. Pray fervently, listen carefully, work diligently, and treat every single day as an exercise in spiritual growth because that's precisely what every day can be—and will be—when you let God help you conquer stress.

SIXTEEN ESSENTIAL STRESS-BUSTING TIPS FOR CHRISTIANS

1. In managing stress, make sure that God is your partner. God is big enough and strong enough to solve any problem you will ever face; so lean on Him.

2. Pray early and often. If you're experiencing too much stress, you should make sure that you're not neglecting your prayer life. Prayer is a powerful tool for managing stress; use it.

3. Get enough rest. Exhaustion is God's way of telling you to slow down. You need rest, and it's up to you (and only you) to make sure that you get it.

4. Don't neglect your daily devotional. If you're serious about beating stress, establish the habit of talking to God first thing every morning.

5. Guard your thoughts. Since your thoughts have the power to magnify stress or decrease it dramatically, you should monitor the quality, the direction, and the veracity of those thoughts.

6. Set priorities carefully. Since you can't do everything, you should make sure that your priorities are appropriate to your circumstances and pleasing to God.

7. Defeat procrastination. Procrastination increases stress; intelligent action decreases it. So if you've acquired the unfortunate habit of putting off unpleasant tasks until the end of the day, it's time to rid yourself of that stress-inducing habit. Instead, do the unpleasant work first and enjoy the rest of the day.

8. Don't engage in needless self-criticism. If you become your own worst critic, you're creating needless stress for yourself and your loved ones.

9. Learn to say no. When your calendar is full, you should learn to say no politely, firmly, and as often as necessary.

10. Reject angry thoughts before they hijack your emotions, not after. Angry thoughts are stress-inducing thoughts. So if you want to defeat stress, you must learn to control your temper before your temper controls you.

11. Don't let temporary setbacks get you down. As you deal with the inevitable stressors of everyday life, don't hit the panic button, don't overreact, and don't give up. To keep things in perspective, remember that genuine success depends upon your relationship with God and His only begotten Son. Period.

12. Don't worry about keeping up with the Joneses. Peer

pressure can be very stressful. So you must focus more on pleasing God and less on pleasing your neighbors.

13. Make peace with the past. Bitterness induces stress while forgiveness and acceptance reduce it. So don't let yesterday use up too much of today.

14. Learn to trust God more and worry less. Needless worry creates needless stress. So when you're troubled, turn your concerns over to the Lord and leave them there.

15. Work hard and leave the rest to God. Do your best and trust God with the rest. And that means accepting the things you cannot change.

16. Make the conscious effort to celebrate life. Remember the familiar words of Psalm 118:24: "This is the day the Lord has made; let us rejoice and be glad in it" (HCSB). Your life can be—and should be—a celebration. But nobody can celebrate for you. It's up to you, and you alone, to praise God for His gifts and to celebrate those gifts throughout the day.

1

BEATING STRESS
ONE DAY AT A TIME

What the Bible Says

*The peace of God, which surpasses all
understanding, will guard your
hearts and minds through Christ Jesus.*

PHILIPPIANS 4:7 NKJV

Life can be stressful—*very* stressful. You live in a world that is brimming with demands, distractions, and deadlines (not to mention temptations, timetables, requirements, and responsibilities). It's no wonder you may feel stressed. So what can you do in response to the stressors of everyday life? A wonderful place to start is by turning things over to God.

Warren Wiersbe writes, "Surrender your mind to the Lord at the beginning of each day." And that's sound advice. When you begin each day with your head bowed and your heart lifted, you are reminded of God's love, His protection, and His commandments. Then you can align your priorities for the coming day with the eternal truths that the Creator has placed upon your heart.

If you've acquired the unfortunate habit of trying to squeeze God into the corners of your life, it's time to reshuffle the items on your to-do list by placing Him first. And if you haven't already done so, form the habit of spending quality time with Him every day. He deserves it, and so do you. So today and every day, make sure that you focus on God and upon His will for your life. And remember that no challenge is too great for Him. Not even yours.

—⁓—

MORE THOUGHTS ABOUT STRESS

*There are very few certainties that touch us all
in this mortal experience, but one of
the absolutes is that we will experience
hardship and stress at some point.*

JAMES DOBSON

*Life is strenuous.
See that your clock does not run down.*

MRS. CHARLES E. COWMAN

*If you're willing to repair your life,
God is willing to help. If you're not willing
to repair your life, God is willing to wait.*

MARIE T. FREEMAN

*Prescription for a happier and healthier life:
resolve to slow down your pace;
learn to say no gracefully;
resist the temptation to chase
after more pleasure, more hobbies,
and more social entanglements.*

JAMES DOBSON

MORE FROM GOD'S WORD

Peace I leave with you;
My peace I give to you;
not as the world gives do I give to you.
Do not let your heart be troubled,
nor let it be fearful.

JOHN 14:27 NASB

This is the day the LORD has made;
we will rejoice and be glad in it.

PSALM 118:24 NKJV

REMEMBER THIS

Beating stress isn't a one-day achievement. To win the battle over life's everyday pressures, you'll need daily doses of perspective, perseverance, practice, and prayer.

GET PRACTICAL

Divide your concerns into two categories: the things you can control and the things you can't. Then focus only on the things you can control and turn everything else over to God. Your job, simply put, is to do your best and to leave the rest up to Him.

2

PRAY ABOUT YOUR STRESSORS

What the Bible Says

*Rejoice always, pray without ceasing,
in everything give thanks; for this is
the will of God in Christ Jesus for you.*

1 THESSALONIANS 5:16–18 NKJV

Want an easy-to-use, highly reliable, readily available antidote to stress? Well, there's a simple solution that's time-tested and guaranteed to help: it's called prayer. The quality and quantity of your prayers will determine, to a surprising extent, the direction of your day *and* the way that you deal with the inevitable challenges of everyday life.

If your prayers have become more a matter of habit than a matter of passion, you're robbing yourself of a deeper relationship with God. And how can you rectify that situation? By praying more frequently and more fervently. When you do, God will shower you with His blessings, His grace, and His love.

Theologian Wayne Oates once admitted, "Many of my prayers are made with my eyes open. You see, it seems I'm always praying about something, and it's not always convenient—or safe—to close my eyes." Dr. Oates understood that God always hears our prayers and that the relative position of our eyelids is of no concern to Him. So instead of trying to do everything on your own, form the habit of asking God for His help. Begin your prayers early in the morning and continue them throughout the day. And remember this: God does answer your prayers, but He's not likely to answer those prayers until you've prayed them.

—⚬—

THE POWER OF PRAYER

*I have witnessed many attitudes
make a positive turnaround through prayer.*

JOHN MAXWELL

*Prayer is not a vending machine
which spits out the appropriate reward.
It is a call to a loving God to relate to us.*

PHILIP YANCEY AND TIM STAFFORD

*God says we don't need to be
anxious about anything;
we just need to pray about everything.*

STORMIE OMARTIAN

Prayer is the answer to every problem there is.

OSWALD CHAMBERS

*Get into the habit of
dealing with God about everything.*

OSWALD CHAMBERS

Pray, and let God worry.

MARTIN LUTHER

MORE FROM GOD'S WORD

I desire therefore that the men
pray everywhere, lifting up holy hands,
without wrath and doubting.
1 Timothy 2:8 NKJV

Is anyone among you suffering?
He should pray.
James 5:13 HCSB

REMEMBER THIS

If you're feeling anxious or worried or both, make sure that you're not neglecting your prayer life. Prayer is a powerful tool for managing stress, and it's a tool that you should use early and often.

GET PRACTICAL

If you want more from life, ask more from God. If you're searching for peace and abundance, ask for God's help—and keep asking—until He answers your prayers. If you sincerely want to rise above the stresses and complications of everyday life, ask for God's help many times each day.

3
RETAIN YOUR BALANCE

What the Bible Says

The one who acquires good sense loves himself;
one who safeguards
understanding finds success.

PROVERBS 19:8 HCSB

Life is a delicate balancing act, a tightrope walk with overcommitment on one side and undercommitment on the other. And it's up to each of us to walk carefully on that rope, not falling prey to pride (which causes us to attempt too much) or to fear (which causes us to attempt too little). God's Word promises us the possibility of abundance, and we are far more likely to experience that abundance when we lead balanced lives.

When you allow yourself to take on too many jobs, you simply can't do all of them well. That means that if you allow yourself to become overcommitted, whether at home, at work, at church, or anywhere in between, you're asking for trouble. So you must learn how to say no to the things you don't have the time or the energy to do.

Of course, sometimes saying no can be tough. Why? Because well-meaning people (like you) genuinely want to help other people. But if you allow yourself to become overworked, you may begin overpromising and underserving; if that happens, you'll disappoint just about everybody, including yourself.

ARE YOU SIMPLY TOO BUSY?

Are you one of those people who is simply too busy for your own good? If so, you're doing everybody a disservice by heaping needless stresses upon yourself and your loved ones.

As an adult, you're responsible for completing your work and managing your free time. And if you're not careful, you may find yourself caught up in a web of time-wasting activities or nonessential obligations. If so, it's helpful to step back and take a fresh look at the way you've been setting priorities.

God offers you a peace that passes human understanding, but He won't force His peace upon you; in order to experience it, you must slow down long enough to sense His presence and His love. Today, as a gift to yourself, to your family, and to your world, slow yourself down, erase a few items from your to-do list, and invite Christ to preside over every aspect of your life. It's the best way to live and the surest path to peace.

—〰—

CONSIDER THIS

Lots of people are clamoring for your attention, your time, and your energy. It's up to you to establish priorities that are important to you, to your family, and to the Lord. And remember, if you don't establish priorities, the world has a way of doing the job for you.

KEEPING YOUR LIFE IN BALANCE

The only way to keep your balance
is to fix your eyes on the One who never changes.
If you gaze too long at your circumstances,
you will become dizzy and confused.

SARAH YOUNG

In the great orchestra we call life,
you have an instrument and a song,
and you owe it to God to play them both sublimely.

MAX LUCADO

Learn to say "no" to the good
so you can say "yes" to the best.

JOHN MAXWELL

As you live your life, you must localize and define it.
You cannot do everything.

PHILLIPS BROOKS

Nothing shapes your life more than the
commitments you choose to make.

RICK WARREN

There are many burned-out people
who think more is always better,
who deem it unspiritual to say no.

SARAH YOUNG

MORE FROM GOD'S WORD

Abundant peace belongs to those who love
Your instruction; nothing makes them stumble.
PSALM 119:165 HCSB

Don't burn out; keep yourselves fueled and aflame.
Be alert servants of the Master,
cheerfully expectant. Don't quit in hard times;
pray all the harder.
ROMANS 12:11–12 MSG

—⚮—

REMEMBER THIS

Unless you can learn to balance your obligations and choose only the most important tasks, you'll find yourself overworked, underappreciated, and stressed out. So your challenge is straightforward: to find the appropriate balance between family, work, fun, rest, exercise, and God.

GET PRACTICAL

Do you feel overwhelmed? Try doing first things first and keeping your focus on high-priority tasks. It's okay to leave some low-priority tasks undone.

4

GET ENOUGH SLEEP

What the Bible Says

Come to Me, all you who labor and are
heavy laden, and I will give you rest.
Take My yoke upon you and learn from Me,
for I am gentle and lowly in heart, and
you will find rest for your souls.
For My yoke is easy and My burden is light.
MATTHEW 11:28–30 NKJV

Physical exhaustion is God's way of telling us to slow down. God expects us to work hard, of course, but He also intends for us to rest. When we fail to take the rest that we need, we do a disservice to ourselves and to our families.

We live in a world that tempts us to stay up late—very late. But too much late-night TV, combined with too little sleep, is a prescription for exhaustion.

As adults, each of us bears a personal responsibility for the general state of our own physical health. Certainly, various aspects of health are beyond our control: illness sometimes strikes even the fittest men and women. But for most of us, physical health is a choice: it is the result of hundreds of small decisions that we make every day of our lives. If we make decisions that promote good health, our bodies respond. But if we fall into bad habits and undisciplined lifestyles, we suffer the consequences.

Are your physical or spiritual batteries running low? Is your energy on the wane? Are your emotions frayed? If so, it's time to turn your thoughts and your prayers to the One who promises to give you rest. And when you're finished, it's probably time to turn off the lights and go to bed!

ABOUT GETTING ENOUGH REST

Life is strenuous.
See that your clock does not run down.
MRS. CHARLES E. COWMAN

Rest and be thankful.
WILLIAM WORDSWORTH

It is a common experience that a problem
difficult at night is resolved in the morning after
the committee of sleep has worked on it.
JOHN STEINBECK

Satan does some of his worst work on
exhausted Christians when nerves
are frayed and their minds are faint.
VANCE HAVNER

Notice what Jesus had to say concerning
those who have wearied themselves
by trying to do things in their own strength:
"Come to me, all you who labor and
are heavy laden, and I will give you rest."
HENRY BLACKABY AND CLAUDE KING

Jesus gives us the ultimate rest,
the confidence we need, to escape
the frustration and chaos of the world around us.

BILLY GRAHAM

—✦—

MORE FROM GOD'S WORD

He said to them, "Come away by yourselves
to a remote place and rest for a while."
For many people were coming and going,
and they did not even have time to eat.

MARK 6:31 HCSB

Return unto thy rest, O my soul;
for the LORD hath dealt bountifully with thee.

PSALM 116:7 KJV

—✦—

REMEMBER THIS

If you're not getting enough sleep, you're inviting stress into your life. You need rest, and it's up to you, and only you, to make sure that you get it.

GET PRACTICAL

Your body, which is a priceless gift from God, needs a sensible amount of sleep each night. So figure out how much sleep you *really* need to feel rested, and then schedule your life—and your viewing habits—accordingly.

5

GUARD YOUR THOUGHTS

What the Bible Says

Guard your heart above all else,
for it is the source of life.

PROVERBS 4:23 HCSB

The level of stress you experience is determined, to a surprising extent, by the direction of your thoughts. If you focus your thoughts and energies on matters that honor your God, your family, and yourself, you will reap rich rewards. But if you focus too intently on the distractions and temptations of our twenty-first-century world, you'll inevitably create more problems than you solve.

What is your focus today? Are you willing to focus your thoughts and energies on God's blessings and upon His will for your life? Or will you turn your thoughts to other things? Before you answer that question, consider this: God created you in His own image, and He wants you to experience joy and abundance. But, God will not force His joy upon you; you must claim it for yourself.

Today, why not focus your thoughts on the joy that is rightfully yours in Christ? Why not take time to celebrate God's glorious creation? And why not trust your hopes instead of your fears? When you do, you'll experience the peace and the power that accrues to those who guard their hearts above all else.

PERSPECTIVE FOR TODAY

If a temporary loss of perspective has left you worried, exhausted, or both, it's time to readjust your thought patterns. Negative thoughts are habit-forming; thankfully, so are positive ones. With practice, you can form the habit of focusing on God's priorities and your possibilities. When you do, you'll soon discover that you will spend less time fretting about your challenges and more time praising Him for His gifts.

When you call upon the Lord and prayerfully seek His will, He will give you wisdom and perspective. When you make God's priorities your priorities, He will direct your steps and calm your fears. So today and every day hereafter, pray for a sense of balance and perspective. And remember: your thoughts are intensely powerful things, so handle them with care.

CONSIDER THIS

Your life is an integral part of God's grand plan. So don't become unduly upset over the minor inconveniences of everyday life, and don't worry too much about today's setbacks—they're temporary.

CHANGING THE DIRECTION OF YOUR THOUGHTS

Change always starts in your mind.
The way you think determines the way you feel,
and the way you feel influences the way you act.

RICK WARREN

Change your thoughts,
and you change your world.

NORMAN VINCENT PEALE

No more imperfect thoughts.
No more sad memories. No more ignorance.
My redeemed body will have a redeemed mind.
Grant me a foretaste of that perfect mind
as You mirror Your thoughts in me today.

JONI EARECKSON TADA

It is the thoughts and intents
of the heart that shape a person's life.

JOHN ELDREDGE

The things we think are the things that feed
our souls. If we think on pure and lovely things,
we shall grow pure and lovely like them;
and the converse is equally true.

HANNAH WHITALL SMITH

MORE FROM GOD'S WORD

*Finally, brothers and sisters, whatever is true,
whatever is noble, whatever is right,
whatever is pure, whatever is lovely,
whatever is admirable—if anything
is excellent or praiseworthy—
think about such things.*

PHILIPPIANS 4:8 NIV

*Guard your heart above all else,
for it is the source of life.*

PROVERBS 4:23 HCSB

REMEMBER THIS

Since your thoughts have the power to increase the amount of stress you feel—or eliminate stress altogether—you should be careful to monitor the quality, the direction, and the veracity of those thoughts.

GET PRACTICAL

Watch what you think. If your inner voice is, in reality, your inner critic, you need to tone down the criticism now. And while you're at it, train yourself to begin thinking thoughts that are more rational, more accepting, and less judgmental.

6

ESTABLISH THE RIGHT PRIORITIES

What the Bible Says

And I pray this: that your love will keep on growing in knowledge and every kind of discernment, so that you can approve the things that are superior and can be pure and blameless in the day of Christ.

PHILIPPIANS 1:9–10 HCSB

On your daily to-do list, all items are not created equal; certain tasks are extremely important while others are not. Therefore it's imperative that you prioritize your daily activities and complete each task in the approximate order of its importance.

The principle of doing first things first is simple in theory but more complicated in practice. Well-meaning family, friends, and coworkers have a way of making unexpected demands upon your time. Furthermore, each day has its own share of minor emergencies, those urgent matters that tend to draw your attention away from more important ones. On paper, prioritizing is simple, but to act upon those priorities in the real world requires maturity, patience, determination, and balance.

If you fail to prioritize your day, life will automatically do the job for you. So your choice is simple: Prioritize or be prioritized. It's a choice that will help determine the quality of your day *and* the quality of your life.

Are you living a balanced life that allows time for worship, for family, for work, for exercise, and a little time left over for yourself? Or do you feel overworked, underappreciated, overwhelmed, and underpaid? If your to-do list is "maxed out" and your energy is on the wane, it's time to restore a sense of balance to your life. You can do so by turning the concerns and the priorities of this day over to God—prayerfully, earnestly, and often. Then, you must listen for His answer . . . and trust the answer He gives.

ESTABLISHING THE RIGHT PRIORITIES

The moment you wake up each morning, all your wishes and hopes for the day rush at you like wild animals. And the first job each morning consists in shoving it all back; in listening to that other voice, taking that other point of view, letting that other, larger, stronger, quieter life coming flowing in.

C. S. Lewis

A disciple is a follower of Christ. That means you take on His priorities as your own. His agenda becomes your agenda. His mission becomes your mission.

Charles Stanley

Things which matter most must never be at the mercy of things which matter least.

Johann Wolfgang von Goethe

Do not let trifles disturb your tranquility of mind. Life is too precious to be sacrificed for the nonessential and transient. Ignore the inconsequential.

GRENVILLE KLEISER

MORE FROM GOD'S WORD

Therefore, whether you eat or drink, or whatever you do, do everything for God's glory.

1 CORINTHIANS 10:31 HCSB

For where your treasure is, there your heart will be also.

LUKE 12:34 HCSB

REMEMBER THIS

Since you can't do everything, you must set priorities. So make sure that your priorities are appropriate to your circumstances and pleasing to God.

GET PRACTICAL

As you're prioritizing your day, ask God to help you sort out big responsibilities from small ones, major problems from minor ones, and important duties from irrelevant ones. When you're faced with a big decision, let God help you decide.

7

LEARN TO SAY NO

What the Bible Says

Get wisdom—how much better it is than gold!
And get understanding—it is preferable to silver.
PROVERBS 16:16 HCSB

If you haven't yet learned to say no—to say it politely, firmly, and often—you're inviting untold stress into your life. Why? Because if you can't say no (when appropriate) to family members, friends, or coworkers, you'll find yourself overcommitted and underappreciated.

If you have trouble standing up for yourself, perhaps you're afraid that you'll be rejected. If that's the case, here's a tip: Don't worry too much about rejection, especially when you're rejected for doing the right things. Pleasing other people is appropriate up to a point. But you must never allow your willingness to please others to interfere with your own good judgment.

God gave you a conscience for a reason: to inform you about the things you need to do as well as the things you don't need to do. It's up to you to follow your conscience wherever it may lead, even if it means making unpopular decisions. Your job, simply put, is to be popular with God, not people.

SAY NO TO OVERCOMMITMENT

The world encourages you to rush full-speed ahead, taking on lots of new commitments, doing many things, but doing few things well. God, on the other hand, encourages you to slow down, to quiet yourself, and to focus on first things first.

How will you organize your life? Will you carve out quiet moments with the Creator? And while you're at it, will you focus your energies and your resources on the most important tasks on your to-do list? Or will you max out your schedule, leaving much of your most important work undone?

Today, slow yourself down and ask God to help you focus on your highest priorities. When you do, you'll discover that time spent with the Father can revolutionize your life.

CONSIDER THIS

You have a right to say no to requests that you consider unreasonable or inconvenient. Don't feel guilty for asserting your right to say no, and don't feel compelled to fabricate excuses for your decisions.

KEEP IT SIMPLE

Nothing becomes an obligation
simply because someone tells you it is.
DAVID SEABURY

How busy we have become . . .
and as a result, how empty!
CHARLES SWINDOLL

The most powerful life is the most simple life.
The most powerful life is the life that knows
where it's going, that knows where the source
of strength is; it is the life that stays free of clutter
and happenstance and hurriedness.
MAX LUCADO

The characteristic of the life of a saint
is essentially elemental simplicity.
OSWALD CHAMBERS

Never assume a responsibility you can't see
through, and when you refuse, be firm.
DAVID SEABURY

MORE FROM GOD'S WORD

*If any of you lacks wisdom, let him ask of God,
who gives to all generously and without reproach,
and it will be given to him.*

JAMES 1:5 NASB

*You, LORD, give true peace to those who depend
on you, because they trust you.*

ISAIAH 26:3 NCV

REMEMBER THIS

Trying to do too much, even if your intentions are pure, is a sure way to invite stress into your home. So if you want to avoid stress, avoid overcommitment.

GET PRACTICAL

Talk to your friends about the drawbacks of being over-committed. Discuss whether it's better to do a few jobs well or many jobs not so well. And talk about the wisdom of saying no to things you simply cannot or should not do.

8

LEARN TO RISE ABOVE ANGER

What the Bible Says

A hot-tempered man stirs up conflict,
but a man slow to anger calms strife.
PROVERBS 15:18 HCSB

Anger is a natural human emotion that is sometimes necessary and appropriate. Even Jesus became angry when confronted with the moneychangers in the temple: "And Jesus entered the temple and drove out all those who were buying and selling in the temple, and overturned the tables of the moneychangers and the seats of those who were selling doves" (Matthew 21:12 NASB).

Righteous indignation is an appropriate response to evil, but God does not intend that anger should rule our lives. Far from it. God intends that we turn away from anger whenever possible and forgive our neighbors just as we seek forgiveness for ourselves.

Life is full of stresses and frustrations, some great and some small. On occasion, you, like Jesus, will confront evil, and when you do, you may respond as He did: vigorously and without reservation.

But, more often than not your frustrations will be of the more mundane variety. As long as you live, you will face countless opportunities to become stressed over small, relatively insignificant events: a traffic jam, a spilled cup of coffee, an inconsiderate comment, a broken promise. When you are tempted to lose your temper over the minor inconveniences of life, don't. Turn away from anger, animosity, bitterness, and regret. Turn instead to God. When you do, you'll be following His commandments and giving yourself a priceless gift: the gift of peace.

—⁓—

BEYOND BITTERNESS

Bitterness is a stress-inducing spiritual sickness. It will consume your soul. It is dangerous to your emotional health. It can destroy you if you let it.

If you are caught up in intense feelings of anger or resentment, you know all too well the destructive power of these emotions.

How can you rid yourself of these feelings? First, you must prayerfully ask God to cleanse your heart. Then you must learn to catch yourself whenever thoughts of bitterness or hatred begin to attack you. Your challenge is this: learn to resist negative thoughts before they hijack your emotions.

Matthew 5:22 issues a stern warning: "But I tell you, if you are angry with a brother or sister, you will be judged. If you say bad things to a brother or sister, you will be judged by the council. And if you call someone a fool, you will be in danger of the fire of hell" (NCV). So we must be slow to anger and quick to forgive, and leave all final judgments to a far more capable authority: our Father in heaven.

CONSIDER THIS

Angry words are dangerous to your emotional and spiritual health, not to mention your relationships. So treat anger as an uninvited guest, and usher it away as quickly—and as quietly—as possible.

AVOID ANGER

When something robs you of your peace of mind, ask yourself if it is worth the energy you are expending on it. If not, then put it out of your mind in an act of discipline. Every time the thought of "it" returns, refuse it.

KAY ARTHUR

Anger is the noise of the soul; the unseen irritant of the heart; the relentless invader of silence.

MAX LUCADO

When you strike out in anger, you may miss the other person, but you will always hit yourself.

JIM GALLERY

Anger breeds remorse in the heart, discord in the home, bitterness in the community, and confusion in the state.

BILLY GRAHAM

For every minute you remain angry,
you give up sixty seconds of peace of mind.
RALPH WALDO EMERSON

—⟊⟊—

MORE FROM GOD'S WORD

Everyone must be quick to hear, slow to speak,
and slow to anger, for man's anger
does not accomplish God's righteousness.
JAMES 1:19–20 HCSB

Do not let the sun go down on your anger,
and do not give the devil an opportunity.
EPHESIANS 4:26–27 NASB

—⟊⟊—

REMEMBER THIS

Angry thoughts are stress-inducing thoughts. So if you want to defeat stress, you must learn to control your temper before your temper controls you.

GET PRACTICAL

Are you holding a grudge? Drop it! Remember, holding a grudge is like letting somebody live rent-free in your brain . . . so don't do it!

9

MANAGING EVERYDAY CRISES

What the Bible Says

Cast your burden on the LORD,
and He will sustain you;
He will never allow the righteous to be shaken.
PSALM 55:22 HCSB

You live in a fast-paced world where one minor crisis after another threatens to snare your attention and distract you from your highest priorities. These everyday crises can hijack your emotions and derail your day if you let them. Occasionally, you'll be faced with a monumental, life-altering emergency, but more often than not, the challenges you'll face will be smaller and less consequential. On most days, the frustrations that annoy you will be relatively minor, yet they still have the power to slow you down and stress you out. Your task, simply put, is to rise serenely and confidently above the minor setbacks that are woven into the fabric of everyday life. You must try, as best you can, to claim control over your emotions before your emotions claim control over you.

Life here on earth can be seen as one test after another, with each minor crisis providing yet another opportunity to stay on the right track or to stray from it. Thankfully, the riddles of everyday living are not too difficult to solve *if* we look for answers in the right places. When we have problems or questions, we should consult our Creator in prayer, we should consult our own consciences, and we should consult a few close friends and family members.

Perhaps Søren Kierkegaard was stating the obvious when he observed, "Life can only be understood backwards; but it must be lived forwards." Taking a forward-looking (and stress-conquering) approach to life means learning the art of addressing everyday problems sensibly, honestly, calmly, and promptly *before* they stress you out, not after.

IN TOUGH TIMES, TRUST GOD

*Our heavenly Father never takes anything
from His children unless he means
to give them something better.*
GEORGE MUELLER

*Often the trials we mourn are really gateways
into the good things we long for.*
HANNAH WHITALL SMITH

*We are all faced with a series of great
opportunities, brilliantly disguised
as unsolvable problems.
Unsolvable without God's wisdom, that is.*
CHARLES SWINDOLL

*After all, a crisis doesn't make a person; it reveals
what a person is made of.*
WARREN WIERSBE

*The size of a person is more important
than the size of the problem.*

JOHN MAXWELL

GOD'S WORD

*God blesses those who patiently endure testing
and temptation. Afterward they will
receive the crown of life that God
has promised to those who love him.*

JAMES 1:12 NLT

The LORD is my shepherd; I shall not want.

PSALM 23:1 KJV

REMEMBER THIS

When you say yes to God, you won't eliminate all stressors from your life, but you will receive His strength to deal with them and His blessings today *and* throughout eternity.

GET PRACTICAL

Never take on a major obligation of any kind without first taking sufficient time to carefully consider whether or not you should commit to it. The bigger the obligation, the more days you should take to decide. If someone presses you for an answer before you are ready, your automatic answer should always be no.

10

MANAGING CHANGE

What the Bible Says

To every thing there is a season, and a time to every purpose under the heaven.

ECCLESIASTES 3:1 KJV

The world, it seems, is changing faster than ever. Technology is changing; our jobs are changing; the economy is changing; and social mores are changing. One thing, however, remains unchanged: our heavenly Father never changes, and neither, for that matter, do His promises.

Even the most faithful Christians are overcome by occasional bouts of fear and doubt. You are no different. But even when you feel very distant from God, remember that God is never distant from you. When you sincerely seek His presence, He will touch your heart, calm your fears, and restore your confidence.

Are you facing unwanted changes? If so, please remember that God is far bigger than any challenge you may face. So instead of worrying about life's inevitable ups and downs (which are temporary), put your faith in the Creator and in His only begotten Son. Commit this verse to memory: "Jesus Christ is the same yesterday, today, and forever" (Hebrews 13:8 NKJV). And while you're at it, remember this: it is precisely because your Lord does not change that you can face your challenges with courage for today and hope for tomorrow.

THOUGHTS ON EMBRACING CHANGE

*Are you on the eve of change? Embrace it.
Accept it. Don't resist it. Change is not only
a part of life, change is a necessary part
of God's strategy. To use us to change the world,
He alters our assignments.*

MAX LUCADO

*We must always change, renew, rejuvenate
ourselves; otherwise we harden.*

JOHANN WOLFGANG VON GOETHE

*If you want things to be different, perhaps
the answer is to become different yourself.*

NORMAN VINCENT PEALE

*Mere change is not growth. Growth is the synthesis
of change and continuity, and where there
is no continuity there is no growth.*

C. S. LEWIS

*The secret of contentment in the midst of change
is found in having roots in the changeless Christ—
the same yesterday, today, and forever.*

ED YOUNG

*The resurrection of Jesus Christ is the power
of God to change history and to change lives.*

BILL BRIGHT

MORE FROM GOD'S WORD

The wise see danger ahead and avoid it,
but fools keep going and get into trouble.
PROVERBS 22:3 NCV

I am the LORD, and I do not change.
MALACHI 3:6 NLT

REMEMBER THIS

The world continues to change, as do we. Change is inevitable—we can either roll with it or be rolled over by it. In order to avoid the latter, we should choose the former.

GET PRACTICAL

Before making a big decision, gather as much information as you can, but don't keep gathering indefinitely. And if a big change is called for, don't be afraid to make it. Sometimes one big leap is better than a thousand baby steps.

11

LEARNING THE ART
OF ACCEPTANCE

What the Bible Says

*Come to terms with God and be at peace;
in this way good will come to you.*
JOB 22:21 HCSB

Sometimes we must accept life on its terms, not our own.
Life has a way of unfolding, not as we will, but as it will. And
occasionally there is precious little we can do to change things.
When events transpire that are beyond our control, we have a
choice: we can either learn the art of acceptance, or we can make
ourselves miserable as we struggle to change the unchangeable.

The American theologian Reinhold Niebuhr composed a
profoundly simple verse that came to be known as the Serenity
Prayer:

> *God, grant me the serenity to accept the things I cannot
> change, the courage to change the things I can, and the
> wisdom to know the difference.*

Niebuhr's words are far easier to recite than they are to live
by. Why? Because most of us want life to unfold in accordance
with our own wishes and timetables. But sometimes God has
other plans.

Author Hannah Whitall Smith observed, "How changed
our lives would be if we could only fly through the days on

wings of surrender and trust!" These words remind us that even when we cannot understand the workings of God, we must trust Him and accept His will. So if you've encountered unfortunate circumstances that are beyond your power to control, accept those circumstances and trust God. When you do, you can be comforted in the knowledge that your Creator is both loving and wise, and that He understands His plans perfectly, even when you do not.

MAKING PEACE WITH YOUR PAST

Because you are human, you may be slow to forget yesterday's disappointments. But if you sincerely seek to focus your hopes and energies on the future, then you must find ways to accept the past, no matter how difficult it may be to do so.

Have you made peace with your past? If so, congratulations. But if you are mired in the quicksand of regret, it's time to plan your escape. How can you do so? By accepting what has been and by trusting God for what will be.

So if you have not yet made peace with the past, today is the day to declare an end to all hostilities. When you do, you can then turn your thoughts to the wondrous promises of God and to the glorious future that He has in store for you.

CONSIDER THIS

When you learn the art of acceptance, you'll worry less and trust God more.

ABOUT THE ART OF ACCEPTANCE

Acceptance is taking from God's hand absolutely anything He gives, looking into His face in trust and thanksgiving, knowing that the confinement of the situation we're in is good and for His glory.

CHARLES SWINDOLL

Surrender to the Lord is not a tremendous sacrifice, not an agonizing performance. It is the most sensible thing you can do.

CORRIE TEN BOOM

He does not need to transplant us into a different field. He transforms the very things that were before our greatest hindrances into the chief and most blessed means of our growth. No difficulties in your case can baffle Him. Put yourself absolutely into His hands, and let Him have His own way with you.

ELISABETH ELLIOT

Ultimately things work out best for those who make the best of the way things work out.

BARBARA JOHNSON

Tomorrow's job is fathered by today's acceptance. Acceptance of what, at least for the moment, you cannot alter.

MAX LUCADO

MORE FROM GOD'S WORD

We can make our plans,
but the Lord determines our steps.
PROVERBS 16:9 NLT

I have learned in whatever state I am,
to be content.
PHILIPPIANS 4:11 NKJV

—⚬—

REMEMBER THIS

It's important to do your best and trust God with the rest. And that means accepting the things you cannot change.

GET PRACTICAL

The past is past, so don't live there. If you're focused on the past, change your focus. If you're living in the past, it's time to stop living there.

12

LEARNING TO BE MORE PATIENT

What the Bible Says

Patience of spirit is better than haughtiness of spirit.
ECCLESIASTES 7:8 NASB

The dictionary defines the word patience as "the ability to be calm, tolerant, and understanding." If that describes you, you can skip the rest of this page. But, if you're like most of us, you'd better keep reading.

For most of us, patience is a hard thing to master. Why? Because we have lots of things we want, and we know precisely when we want them: now. But our Father in heaven has other ideas. The Bible teaches that we must learn to wait patiently for the things that He has in store for us, even when waiting is difficult.

We live in an imperfect world inhabited by imperfect people. Sometimes we inherit troubles from others, and sometimes we create troubles for ourselves. On other occasions, we see other people "moving ahead" in the world, and we want to move ahead with them. So we become impatient with ourselves, with our circumstances, and even with our Creator.

Psalm 37:7 commands us to "rest in the LORD, and wait patiently for Him" (NKJV).

So the next time you find yourself impatiently drumming your fingers as you wait for a quick resolution to the challenges of everyday living, take a deep breath and ask God for patience.

Be still before your heavenly Father and trust His timetable; it's the peaceful way to live.

—–∭–—

BE PATIENT

All things pass. Patience attains all it strives for.
ST. TERESA OF AVILA

Patience and diligence, like faith, move mountains.
WILLIAM PENN

As we wait on God, He helps us use the winds
of adversity to soar above our problems.
As the Bible says, "Those who wait on the Lord . . .
shall mount up with wings like eagles."
BILLY GRAHAM

Two signposts of faith:
"Slow Down" and "Wait Here."
CHARLES STANLEY

When we read of the great biblical leaders,
we see that it was not uncommon for God to ask
them to wait, not just a day or two, but for years,
until God was ready for them to act.
GLORIA GAITHER

God never hurries. There are no deadlines against which He must work. To know this is to quiet our spirits and relax our nerves.

A. W. TOZER

—⟁—

MORE FROM GOD'S WORD

A person's wisdom yields patience; it is to one's glory to overlook an offense.

PROVERBS 19:11 NIV

Better to be patient than powerful; better to have self-control than to conquer a city.

PROVERBS 16:32 NLT

—⟁—

REMEMBER THIS

Impatience creates stress. Patience relieves it. If you want to become a more peaceful person, you'll need to become a more patient person.

GET PRACTICAL

If you think you've lost control over your emotions, don't make big decisions, don't strike out against anybody, and don't speak out in anger. Count to ten (or more) and take "time out" from your situation until you calm down.

13

DEFEATING PROCRASTINATION

What the Bible Says

*When you make a vow to God,
don't delay fulfilling it, because He does not
delight in fools. Fulfill what you vow.*
ECCLESIASTES 5:4 HCSB

Procrastination and stress are traveling companions, so it's up to you to figure out how to defeat procrastination before it defeats you.

If you find yourself bound by the chains of procrastination, ask yourself what you're waiting for—or more accurately what you're afraid of—and why. As you examine the emotional roadblocks that have heretofore blocked your path, you may discover that you're waiting for the "perfect" moment, that instant in time when you feel neither afraid nor anxious. But in truth, perfect moments like these are few and far between.

So stop waiting for the perfect moment or the comfortable moment or the easy moment, and focus instead on finding the *right* moment to do what needs to be done. Then trust God and get busy. When you do, you'll discover that you and the Father, working together, can accomplish great things—and that you can accomplish them sooner rather than later.

Once you acquire the habit of doing what needs to be done when it needs to be done, you will avoid untold trouble, worry, and stress. So learn to overcome procrastination by paying less attention to your fears and more attention to your responsibilities. God has created a world that punishes procrastinators and rewards people who "do it now." In other words, life doesn't procrastinate. Neither should you.

DO IT NOW!

I've found that the worst thing I can do when it comes to any kind of potential pressure situation is to put off dealing with it.

JOHN MAXWELL

Better to do something imperfectly than to do nothing flawlessly.

ROBERT SCHULLER

Every time you refuse to face up to life and its problems, you weaken your character.

E. STANLEY JONES

The fear of attempting something big immobilizes people. To begin a task is usually the toughest step.

JOHN MAXWELL

Not now becomes never.

MARTIN LUTHER

*Never fail to do something because
you don't feel like it. Sometimes you just have
to do it now, and you'll feel like it later.*

MARIE T. FREEMAN

—⟋⟍—

MORE FROM GOD'S WORD

*But prove yourselves doers of the word,
and not merely hearers who delude themselves.*

JAMES 1:22 NASB

*Therefore, with your minds ready for action,
be serious and set your hope completely
on the grace to be brought to you
at the revelation of Jesus Christ.*

1 PETER 1:13 HCSB

—⟋⟍—

REMEMBER THIS

Procrastination increases stress; intelligent action decreases it. Act accordingly.

GET PRACTICAL

It's easy to put off unpleasant tasks until "later." A far better strategy is this: do the unpleasant work first so you can enjoy the rest of the day.

14

KEEPING UP WITH THE JONESES? DON'T DO IT!

What the Bible Says

For where your treasure is,
there your heart will be also.

Luke 12:34 NKJV

As a member in good standing in this highly competitive, twenty-first-century society, you know that the demands and expectations of everyday living can seem burdensome, even overwhelming at times. Keeping up with the Joneses can become a stress-inducing, ego-deflating, twenty-four-hour-a-day job *if* you let it. A better strategy, of course, is to stop trying to please the neighbors and to concentrate, instead, on pleasing God.

Perhaps you have set your goals high; if so, congratulations! You're willing to dream big dreams, and that's a very good thing. But as you consider your life's purpose, don't allow your quest for excellence to interfere with the spiritual journey that God has planned for you.

As a Christian, your instructions are clear: you must try to please God first and always. And how do you please Him? By walking with His Son and by obeying His commandments. All other concerns—including, but not limited to, keeping up appearances—are of relatively little importance. So if you're making purchases in order to impress the Joneses, or anybody else for that matter, stop it! Pleasing God (by leading a sensible, moderate life that gives you time and energy to focus on Him) is more important than impressing your neighbors—*far* more important.

—⁓—

BEYOND ENVY

Because we are frail, imperfect human beings, we are sometimes envious of others. But God's Word warns us that envy is sin. Thus, we must guard ourselves against the natural tendency to feel resentment and jealousy when other people experience good fortune. As believers, we have absolutely no reason to be envious of any people on earth. After all, as Christians we are already recipients of the greatest gift in all creation: God's grace. We have been promised the gift of eternal life through God's only begotten Son, and we must count that gift as our most precious possession.

So here's a simple suggestion that is guaranteed to reduce stress and increase happiness: fill your heart with God's love, God's promises, and God's Son; and when you do so, there's no room left for envy, hatred, bitterness, or regret.

—⁓—

CONSIDER THIS

You should own your possessions, not vice versa. Too much stuff doesn't eliminate stress. In fact, having too much stuff actually creates stress.

DON'T TRY TO
KEEP UP WITH THE JONESES

Comparison is the root of all feelings of inferiority.
JAMES DOBSON

*Ambition! We must be careful what
we mean by it. If it means the desire
to get ahead of other people—which is what
I think it does mean—then it is bad.
If it simply means wanting to do a thing well,
then it is good. It isn't wrong for an actor
to want to act his part as well as it can possibly
be acted, but the wish to have his name in bigger
type than the other actors is a bad one.*
C. S. LEWIS

*People who constantly, and fervently,
seek the approval of others live with an identity
crisis. They don't know who they are, and they
are defined by what others think of them.*
CHARLES STANLEY

*If you desire many things,
many things will seem but a few.*
BEN FRANKLIN

Less is more.
LUDWIG MIES VAN DER ROHE

MORE FROM GOD'S WORD

No one can serve two masters. For you will hate one and love the other; you will be devoted to one and despise the other. You cannot serve God and be enslaved to money.

Luke 16:13 NLT

We brought nothing into the world, so we can take nothing out. But, if we have food and clothes, we will be satisfied with that.

1 Timothy 6:7–8 NCV

REMEMBER THIS

For children and adults alike, peer pressure can be very stressful. Your job, therefore, is to worry more about pleasing your Creator and less about pleasing your friends or neighbors.

GET PRACTICAL

Envy is a sin—a sin that robs you of contentment and increases stress. Today and every day, you must steadfastly refuse to let feelings of envy invade your thoughts or your heart.

15

THE POWER OF A CHEERFUL DISPOSITION

What the Bible Says

A cheerful heart has a continual feast.

PROVERBS 15:15 HCSB

Cheerfulness is a wonderful antidote to stress. And as believers who trust God's promises, why shouldn't we be cheerful? The answer, of course, is that we have every reason to honor our Lord with joy in our hearts, smiles on our faces, and words of celebration on our lips.

Few things in life are more sad, or, for that matter, more absurd than the sight of grumpy Christians trudging unhappily through life. Christ promises us lives of abundance and joy if we accept His love and His grace. Yet sometimes, even the most faithful among us are beset by fits of ill temper and frustration. During these moments, we may not feel like turning our thoughts and prayers to God, but that's precisely what we should do.

Mrs. Charles E. Cowman, the author of the classic devotional text *Streams in the Desert*, wrote, "Two wings are necessary to lift our souls toward God: prayer and praise. Prayer asks. Praise accepts the answer." That's why we should find the time to lift our concerns to the Father in prayer. And then we should praise Him for all that He has done. When we do, we simply can't stay stressed for long.

THE REWARDS OF CHEERFULNESS

Christ can put a spring in your step and a thrill in your heart. Optimism and cheerfulness are products of knowing Christ.

BILLY GRAHAM

We may run, walk, stumble, drive, or fly, but let us never lose sight of the reason for the journey, or miss a chance to see a rainbow on the way.

GLORIA GAITHER

When we bring sunshine into the lives of others, we're warmed by it ourselves. When we spill a little happiness, it splashes on us.

BARBARA JOHNSON

God is good, and heaven is forever. And if those two facts don't cheer you up, nothing will.

MARIE T. FREEMAN

The people whom I have seen succeed best in life have always been cheerful and hopeful people who went about their business with a smile on their faces.

CHARLES KINGSLEY

*Be assured, my dear friend, that it is no joy to God
in seeing you with a dreary countenance.*

C. H. SPURGEON

MORE FROM GOD'S WORD

*Rejoice always, pray without ceasing,
in everything give thanks; for this
is the will of God in Christ Jesus for you.*

1 THESSALONIANS 5:16–18 NKJV

*This is the day that the LORD has made.
Let us rejoice and be glad today!*

PSALM 118:24 NCV

REMEMBER THIS

Stress and cheerfulness don't usually coexist in the same human heart.

GET PRACTICAL

If you can't see the joy and humor in everyday life, you're not paying attention to the right things. Remember the do-nut-maker's creed: "As you travel through life, brother, whatever be your goal, keep your eye upon the donut, and not upon the hole."

16

LISTEN TO YOUR CONSCIENCE

What the Bible Says

*Now the goal of our instruction is love
that comes from a pure heart,
a good conscience, and a sincere faith.*

1 TIMOTHY 1:5 HCSB

God gave you a conscience for a very good reason: to make your path conform to His will. Billy Graham correctly observed, "Most of us follow our conscience as we follow a wheelbarrow. We push it in front of us in the direction we want to go." To do so, of course, is a profound mistake. Yet all of us, on occasion, have failed to listen to the voice that God planted in our hearts, and all of us have suffered the stressful consequences of our actions.

Few things in life are more vexing than a guilty conscience. When we knowingly behave in ways that are contrary to our values, we scatter seeds of discontent and sorrow. And if we're not careful, those seeds may grow into fully formed, stress-inducing crises.

Wise Christians make it a practice to listen carefully to the quiet internal voice that speaks wisdom and truth. Count yourself among that number. When your conscience speaks, listen and learn. In all likelihood, God is trying to get His message through. And in all likelihood, it is a message that you desperately need to hear.

FOLLOW YOUR CONSCIENCE

*God speaks to us through our conscience. This may
be a quiet voice that will not let us
go until we do what we know is right. We must
never silence that inner voice.*

BILLY GRAHAM

*Your conscience is your alarm system.
It's your protection.*

CHARLES STANLEY

*It is neither safe nor prudent to do anything
against one's conscience.*

MARTIN LUTHER

*God desires that we become spiritually healthy
enough through faith to have a conscience that
rightly interprets the work of the Holy Spirit.*

BETH MOORE

A good conscience is a continual feast.

FRANCIS BACON

Conscience is the perfect interpreter of life.

KARL BARTH

MORE FROM GOD'S WORD

So I strive always to keep my conscience
clear before God and man.
ACTS 24:16 NIV

Let us come near to God with a sincere heart
and a sure faith, because we have been made
free from a guilty conscience, and our bodies
have been washed with pure water.
HEBREWS 10:22 NCV

REMEMBER THIS

Whenever you listen carefully to your conscience (and obey it), you make your world (and your heart) a less stressful place.

GET PRACTICAL

If you feel your emotional temperature rising, step back from the situation, take a few deep breaths, calm yourself down, and think before you act. The more stressful the situation, the more carefully you should listen to your conscience.

17

FORGIVENESS MATTERS

What the Bible Says

*Be kind to one another, tender-hearted,
forgiving each other, just as God
in Christ also has forgiven you.*

EPHESIANS 4:32 NASB

It has been said that life is an exercise in forgiveness Christ understood the importance of forgiveness when He commanded, "Love your enemies and pray for those who persecute you" (Matthew 5:44 NIV). But sometimes forgiveness is difficult.

When we have been injured or embarrassed, we feel the urge to strike back and to hurt the ones who have hurt us. Christ instructs us to do otherwise. Christians are taught that forgiveness is an integral part of God's plan for our lives. In short, we are commanded to weave the thread of forgiveness into the very fabric of our lives.

Today, as you go about your daily affairs, remember that you have already been forgiven by your heavenly Father. Now it's your turn to forgive others. If you bear bitterness against anyone, take your bitterness to God and leave it there. If you are angry, pray for God's healing hand to calm your spirit. If you are troubled by some past injustice, read God's Word and remember His commandment to forgive. When you forgive the people who have hurt you, you'll discover that a heavy burden has been lifted from your shoulders. And you'll discover that, although forgiveness is indeed difficult, with God's help all things are possible.

GOD COMMANDS US TO FORGIVE

*Learning how to forgive and forget is one
of the secrets of a happy Christian life.*

WARREN WIERSBE

*I have always found that mercy
bears richer fruits than strict justice.*

ABRAHAM LINCOLN

*We must learn to regard people less
in the light of what they do or omit to do,
and more in light of what they suffer.*

DIETRICH BONHOEFFER

*Nobody is perfect. Look for the good in others.
Forget the rest.*

BARBARA BUSH

*Better by far you should forget and smile
than you should remember and be sad.*

CHRISTINA ROSSETTI

It is in pardoning that we are pardoned.

ST. FRANCIS OF ASSISI

MORE FROM GOD'S WORD

Judge not, and you shall not be judged.
Condemn not, and you shall not be condemned.
Forgive, and you will be forgiven.
LUKE 6:37 NKJV

Above all, love each other deeply,
because love covers a multitude of sins.
1 PETER 4:8 NIV

—⚬⚬—

REMEMBER THIS

Forgiveness is its own reward. Bitterness is its own punishment. Until you learn how to forgive, you'll stay locked inside a stress-inducing emotional prison of your own making.

GET PRACTICAL

When it comes to the task of forgiving others, God wants you to be relentless. He wants you to start forgiving now and keep forgiving until it sticks. So, if you're having trouble forgiving someone, pray about it, and keep praying until the Lord answers your prayer.

18

GRATITUDE
REDUCES STRESS

What the Bible Says

Give thanks to the Lord, for He is good;
His faithful love endures forever.
PSALM 106:1 HCSB

God has blessed us beyond measure, and we owe Him everything, including our constant praise. That's why thanksgiving should become a habit, a regular part of our daily routines. When we slow down and express our gratitude to the One who made us, we enrich our own lives and the lives of those around us.

Dietrich Bonhoeffer observed, "It is only with gratitude that life becomes rich." These words most certainly apply to you. God sent His only Son to die for you, and He has given you the priceless gifts of eternal love and eternal life. You, in turn, should approach your heavenly Father with reverence and gratitude.

Are you a thankful person? Do you appreciate the gifts that the Lord has given you? Do you demonstrate your gratitude by being a faithful steward of those gifts? You most certainly should be thankful. After all, when you stop to think about it, God has given you more blessings than you can count. So the question of the day is this: will you invest some time thanking your heavenly Father, or will you spend all your time and energy doing other things?

MORE FROM GOD'S WORD

Enter into His gates with thanksgiving,
and into His courts with praise.
Be thankful to Him, and bless His name.
For the Lᴏʀᴅ is good; His mercy is everlasting,
and His truth endures to all generations.

Pꜱᴀʟᴍ 100:4–5 NKJV

I will thank Yahweh with all my heart;
I will declare all Your wonderful works.
I will rejoice and boast about You;
I will sing about Your name, Most High.

Pꜱᴀʟᴍ 9:1–2 HCSB

REMEMBER THIS

If you want to overcome the stresses of everyday life, a great way to start is by spending more time thanking God and praising Him for gifts too numerous to count.

GET PRACTICAL

If you're simply too stressed to celebrate life, try counting your blessings one by one. When you do, you won't stay stressed for long.

19

WHEN PEOPLE BEHAVE BADLY

What the Bible Says

Don't answer a fool according to his foolishness or you'll be like him yourself.

PROVERBS 26:4 HCSB

All of us can be grumpy, hardheaded, and difficult to deal with at times. And all of us, from time to time, encounter folks who behave in the same way, or worse. When you encounter a difficult person, it's up to you, and nobody else, to maintain your peace of mind. Of course, the other person's prickly personality may make your job harder. After all, difficult people have a way of riling our emotions and distorting our thoughts. But with God's help, and with a little common sense, we can find peace amid the emotional storm.

Life is too short to allow another person's problematic personality to invade your psyche and ruin your day. But because human emotions are contagious, there's always the danger that you'll be drawn into the other person's mental state, with predictably negative consequences.

A far better strategy is to step back from the stressful situation, to say a silent prayer, and to ask God to help you retain a sense of calm. When you do, He'll answer your prayer, the storm will pass, and you'll be glad you retained your emotional stability, even when people around you were losing theirs.

ABOUT NEGATIVE BEHAVIOR

*We are all fallen creatures
and all very hard to live with.*

C. S. LEWIS

*Whenever you catch yourself starting
to complain about someone, you would do
well to turn your thoughts inward and inspect
your own thoughts and deeds.*

ST. STEPHEN OF MURET

*Bear with the faults of others as you
would have them bear with yours.*

PHILLIPS BROOKS

*Avoid arguments, but when a negative
attitude is expressed, counter it
with a positive and optimistic opinion.*

NORMAN VINCENT PEALE

*You are justified in avoiding people who
send you from their presence with less
hope and strength to cope with life's
problems than when you met them.*

ELLA WHEELER WILCOX

*A keen sense of humor helps us to overlook the
unbecoming, understand the unconventional,
tolerate the unpleasant, overcome the
unexpected, and outlast the unbearable.*

BILLY GRAHAM

MORE FROM GOD'S WORD

Bad temper is contagious—don't get infected.
PROVERBS 22:25 MSG

Stay away from a foolish man;
you will gain no knowledge from his speech.
PROVERBS 14:7 HCSB

—⚍—

REMEMBER THIS

Sometimes people can be difficult, but it doesn't pay to get angry—your job is to be as understanding as possible. And while you're at it, remember that God wants you to forgive other folks, just like He forgives you.

GET PRACTICAL

Don't allow yourself to become caught up in another person's emotional outbursts. If someone is ranting, raving, or worse, you have the right to get up and leave. Instead of adding your own emotional energy to the outburst, you should make the conscious effort to remain calm. And remember this: part of remaining calm may be leaving the scene of the argument.

20

MANAGING STRESS IN TOUGH TIMES

What the Bible Says

For whatever is born of God overcomes the world. And this is the victory that has overcome the world—our faith.

1 JOHN 5:4 NKJV

As life here on earth unfolds, all of us encounter occasional stresses and setbacks. They are simply a fact of life, and none of us are exempt. When tough times arrive, we may be forced to rearrange our plans and our priorities. But even on our darkest days, we must remember that God's love remains constant.

The fact that we encounter adversity is not nearly as important as the way we choose to deal with it. We have a clear choice: we can either begin the difficult work of tackling our troubles . . . or not. When we summon the courage to look Old Man Trouble squarely in the eye, he usually blinks. But if we refuse to address our problems, even the smallest stresses have a way of growing into king-size catastrophes.

As believers, we know that God loves us and that He will protect us. In times of hardship, He will comfort us; in times of sorrow, He will dry our tears. When we are troubled or weak or sorrowful, God is always with us. We must build our lives on the rock that cannot be shaken; we must trust in God. And then we must get on with the hard work of tackling our problems . . . because if we don't, who will? Or should?

WHEN TIMES ARE TOUGH

Adversity is always unexpected and unwelcomed. It is an intruder and a thief, and yet in the hands of God, adversity becomes the means through which His supernatural power is demonstrated.

CHARLES STANLEY

Every misfortune, every failure, every loss may be transformed. God has the power to transform all misfortunes into "God-sends."

MRS. CHARLES E. COWMAN

Often the trials we mourn are really gateways into the good things we long for.

HANNAH WHITALL SMITH

You'll never know that God is all you need until God is all you've got.

RICK WARREN

God will not permit any troubles to come upon us unless He has a specific plan by which great blessing can come out of the difficulty.

PETER MARSHALL

MORE FROM GOD'S WORD

We are hard-pressed on every side, yet not crushed; we are perplexed, but not in despair.
2 CORINTHIANS 4:8 NKJV

The LORD is my rock, my fortress, and my deliverer, my God, my mountain where I seek refuge. My shield, the horn of my salvation, my stronghold, my refuge, and my Savior.
2 SAMUEL 22:2–3 HCSB

REMEMBER THIS

When tough times arrive, you should work as if everything depended upon you and pray as if everything depended upon God.

GET PRACTICAL

Do you lack confidence? If so, pay careful attention to the direction of your thoughts. And while you're at it, pay careful attention to the promises contained in God's Holy Word. Remember: the more you trust God, the more confident, and less stressed, you will become.

21

AVOIDING THE TRAP OF SELF-CRITICISM

What the Bible Says

You formed my inward parts; You covered me in my mother's womb. I will praise You, for I am fearfully and wonderfully made; marvelous are Your works.

PSALM 139:13–14 NKJV

Are you your own worst critic? And in response to that criticism, are you constantly trying to transform yourself into a person who meets society's expectations? If so, it's time to become a little more understanding of the person you see whenever you look into the mirror.

Being patient with other people can be difficult. But sometimes, we find it even more difficult to be patient with ourselves. We have high expectations and lofty goals. We want to receive God's blessings now, not later. And, of course, we want our lives to unfold according to our own wishes and our own timetables—not God's. Yet throughout the Bible, we are instructed that patience is the companion of wisdom. Proverbs 16:32 teaches us that "patience is better than strength" (NCV). God's message, then, is clear: we must be patient with all people—including ourselves.

The Bible affirms the importance of self-acceptance by exhorting believers to love others as they love themselves (Matthew 22:39). Furthermore, the Bible teaches that when we genuinely open our hearts to Him, God accepts us just as we are. And if He accepts us—faults and all—then who are we to believe otherwise?

—–∿∿–—

DEFEATING NEGATIVITY

From experience, we know that it is easy to criticize others. And we know that it is usually far easier to find faults than to find solutions. Still, the urge to criticize others remains a powerful temptation for most of us.

Negativity is highly contagious: we give it to others who in turn give it back to us. This stress-inducing cycle can be broken only by positive thoughts, heartfelt prayers, encouraging words, and meaningful acts of kindness.

As thoughtful servants of a loving God, we have no valid reasons—and no legitimate excuses—to be negative. So when we are tempted to be overly critical of others, or unfairly critical of ourselves, we must use the transforming power of God's love to break the chains of negativity. We must defeat negativity before negativity defeats us.

—–∿∿–—

CONSIDER THIS

God knows that you're a wonderful, miraculous, one-of-a-kind creation. You should know it too.

ABOUT BEING KIND TO YOURSELF

*Do not lose courage in considering
your own imperfections.*

St. Francis of Sales

*Being loved by Him whose opinion matters
most gives us the security to risk loving,
too—even loving ourselves.*

Gloria Gaither

*I think that if God forgives us we might forgive
ourselves. Otherwise it is almost like setting
up ourselves as a higher tribunal than Him.*

C. S. Lewis

*He who is able to love himself
is able to love others also.*

Paul Tillich

*Do not wish to be anything but what you are,
and try to be that perfectly.*

St. Francis of Sales

*You have to be what you are.
Whatever you are, that's what you gotta be.*

Johnny Cash

MORE FROM GOD'S WORD

And we have known and believed the love that God has for us. God is love, and he who abides in love abides in God, and God in him.

1 John 4:16 NKJV

We love him, because he first loved us.

1 John 4:19 KJV

REMEMBER THIS

If you become your own worst critic, you're creating needless stress for yourself and your loved ones. Constant self-criticism is bad for your spiritual, mental, and emotional health.

GET PRACTICAL

Negative thinking breeds more negative thinking. So it's imperative that you catch yourself when you're being overly negative and put an end to those thoughts before they have a chance to grow.

22

TAKING CARE
OF YOUR BODY

What the Bible Says

*Don't you know that your body is a sanctuary of
the Holy Spirit who is in you, whom you have from
God? You are not your own, for you were bought
at a price. Therefore glorify God in your body.*

1 CORINTHIANS 6:19–20 HCSB

Poor physical health and stress often go hand in hand. That's one reason (but certainly not the only reason) that you should place a high priority on caring for the only body that you'll ever own in this lifetime.

God's Word has much to say about every aspect of your life, including your health. If you face personal health challenges that seem almost insoluble, have faith and seek God's wisdom. If you can't seem to get yourself on a sensible diet or on a program of regular physical exercise, consult God's teachings. If your approach to your physical or emotional health has, up to this point, been undisciplined, ask God for the strength to do what you know is right.

The Lord has given you the Holy Bible for the purpose of knowing His promises, His power, His commandments, His wisdom, His love, and His Son. As you seek to improve the state of your own health, study God's teachings and apply them to your life. When you do, you'll quickly discover that God has the power to change everything, including you.

SENSIBLE EXERCISE REDUCES STRESS

How much exercise is right for you? That's a decision that you should make in consultation with your physician. But make no mistake: if you sincerely desire to be a thoughtful caretaker of the body that God has given you, exercise is important.

Once you begin a regular exercise program, you'll discover that the benefits to you are not only physical but also psychological. Regular exercise allows you to build your muscles while you're clearing your head and lifting your spirits.

So if you've been taking your body for granted, today is a wonderful day to change. You can start slowly, perhaps with a brisk walk around the block. As your stamina begins to build, so too will your sense of satisfaction. And you'll be comforted by the knowledge that you've done your part to protect and preserve the precious body that God has entrusted to your care.

CONSIDER THIS

With God's help, you can treat your body as the priceless, one-of-a-kind gift that it most certainly is. Your job, simply put, is to ask Him for the strength and the wisdom to treat your body like His temple.

MORE THOUGHTS ABOUT HEALTH

People are funny. When they are young,
they will spend their health to get wealth.
Later, they will gladly pay all they
have trying to get their health back.

JOHN MAXWELL

Be sober and temperate, and you will be healthy.
Be in general virtuous, and you will be happy.

BEN FRANKLIN

You can't buy good health at the doctor's office—
you've got to earn it for yourself.

MARIE T. FREEMAN

Be careful to preserve your health.
It is a trick of the devil, which he employs
to deceive good souls, to incite them
to do more than they are able, in order that
they may no longer be able to do anything.

ST. VINCENT DE PAUL

I saw few die of hunger;
of eating, a hundred thousand.

BEN FRANKLIN

MORE FROM GOD'S WORD

The L<small>ORD</small> will take away from thee all sickness.
D<small>EUTERONOMY</small> 7:15 KJV

I am the L<small>ORD</small> who heals you.
E<small>XODUS</small> 15:26 NCV

REMEMBER THIS

A healthy lifestyle reduces stress just as surely as an unhealthy lifestyle increases stress. And since your body is a gift from God, you should treat it with the care it deserves.

GET PRACTICAL

Physical exercise helps relieve stress. And remember that physical, emotional, and spiritual fitness are part of God's plan for you. But it's up to you to make certain that a healthy lifestyle is a fundamental part of your plan too.

23

REDUCING STRESS WITH A POSITIVE ATTITUDE

What the Bible Says

Finally brothers, whatever is true, whatever is honorable, whatever is just, whatever is pure, whatever is lovely, whatever is commendable— if there is any moral excellence and if there is any praise—dwell on these things.

PHILIPPIANS 4:8 HCSB

The Christian life is a cause for celebration, but sometimes we don't feel much like celebrating. In fact, when the weight of the world seems to bear down upon our shoulders, celebration may be the last thing on our minds . . . but it shouldn't be. As God's children, we are all blessed beyond measure on good days and bad. Today is a nonrenewable resource; once it's gone, it's gone forever. We should give thanks for this day while using it for the glory of God.

What will be your attitude today? Will you be fearful, angry, bored, or worried? Will you be cynical, bitter, or pessimistic? If so, God wants to have a little talk with you.

God wants you to experience joyful abundance, but He will not force you to experience His joy and His peace. You must claim them for yourself.

ANXIOUS?

We live in a fast-paced, stress-inducing, anxiety-filled society that oftentimes seems to shift beneath our feet. Sometimes trusting God is difficult, especially when we become caught up in the incessant demands of an anxious world.

When you feel stressed to the breaking point—and you will—return your thoughts to God's love and God's promises. And as you confront the challenges of everyday living, turn all of your concerns over to Him.

The same God who created the universe will comfort and guide you if you ask Him, so ask Him. Then watch in amazement as your anxieties begin to fade and your spirits begin to rise.

MORE THOUGHTS ABOUT ATTITUDE

Attitude is more important than the past, than education, than money, than circumstances, than what people do or say. It is more important than appearance, giftedness, or skill.

CHARLES SWINDOLL

You've heard the saying, "Life is what you make it." That means we have a choice. We can choose to have a life full of frustration and fear, but we can just as easily choose one of joy and contentment.

DENNIS SWANBERG

Each of us makes his own weather.
FULTON J. SHEEN

Your attitude, not your aptitude,
will determine your altitude.
ZIG ZIGLAR

MORE FROM GOD'S WORD

A merry heart makes a cheerful countenance.
PROVERBS 15:13 NKJV

You must have the same attitude
that Christ Jesus had.
PHILIPPIANS 2:5 NLT

REMEMBER THIS

As the old saying goes, your attitude determines your altitude. And your attitude also determines your stress level. So think—and act—accordingly.

GET PRACTICAL

Today, create a positive attitude by focusing on opportunities, not roadblocks. Of course you may have experienced disappointments in the past, and you will undoubtedly experience some setbacks in the future. But don't invest large amounts of energy focusing on past misfortunes. Instead, look to the future with optimism and hope.

24

BEYOND FAILURE

What the Bible Says

*A righteous man may fall
seven times and rise again.*

PROVERBS 24:16 NKJV

The occasional disappointments and failures of life are inevitable. Such setbacks are simply the price that we must pay for our willingness to take risks as we follow our dreams. But even when we encounter bitter disappointments, we must never lose faith.

The reassuring words of Hebrews 10:36 remind us that when we persevere, we will eventually receive that which God has promised. What's required is perseverance, not perfection.

When we encounter the inevitable difficulties and stresses of life here on earth, God stands ready to protect us. Our responsibility, of course, is to ask Him for protection. When we call upon Him in heartfelt prayer, He will answer—in His own time and according to His own plan. And while we are waiting for God's plans to unfold and for His healing touch to restore us, we can be comforted in the knowledge that our Creator can overcome any obstacle, even if we cannot.

The next time you experience failure, don't despair and don't be afraid to try Plan B. Consider every setback as an opportunity to choose a different, more appropriate path. Have faith that God may indeed be leading you in an entirely different direction—a direction of His choosing. And as you take your next step, remember that what looks like a dead end to you may, in fact, be the fast lane according to God.

ABOUT DEALING WITH FAILURE

Goals are worth setting and worth missing. We learn from non-successes.

BILL BRIGHT

*Our problem isn't that we've failed.
Our problem is that we haven't failed enough.
We haven't been brought low enough
to learn what God wants us to learn.*

CHARLES SWINDOLL

*Success or failure can be pretty well predicted
by the degree to which the heart is fully in it.*

JOHN ELDREDGE

*God sometimes permits us to experience
humiliating defeats in order to test our faith and to
reveal to us what's really going on in our hearts.*

WARREN WIERSBE

*Failure is one of life's most powerful teachers.
How we handle our failures determines whether
we're going to simply "get by" in life or "press on."*

BETH MOORE

If you're willing to repair your life,
God is willing to help. If you're not willing
to repair your life, God is willing to wait.

MARIE T. FREEMAN

MORE FROM GOD'S WORD

As for you, be strong; don't be discouraged,
for your work has a reward.

2 CHRONICLES 15:7 HCSB

Weeping may endure for a night,
but joy comes in the morning.

PSALM 30:5 NKJV

REMEMBER THIS

If you're experiencing setbacks or hardships, don't hit the panic button, and don't overreact. Failure isn't permanent unless you fail to get back up.

GET PRACTICAL

Don't spend too much time asking, "Why me, Lord?" Instead ask, "What now, Lord?" and then get to work. When you do, you'll feel much better.

25

GENUINE WORSHIP REDUCES STRESS

What the Bible Says

*I rejoiced with those who said to me,
"Let us go to the house of the LORD."*
PSALM 122:1 HCSB

To worship God is a privilege, but it's a privilege that far too many of us forego. Instead of praising our Creator seven days a week, we worship on Sunday mornings (if at all) and spend the rest of the week focusing on other things.

Whenever we become distracted by worldly pursuits that put God in second place, we inevitably pay the price of our misplaced priorities. A better strategy, of course, is to worship Him every day of the week, beginning with a regular early-morning devotional.

Every new day provides another opportunity to worship the Creator with grateful hearts and helping hands. And each day offers another chance to support the church He created. When we do so we bless others, and we are blessed by the One who sent His Son so that we might have eternal life.

If you really want to know God, worship Him seven days a week, not just on Sunday. When you do, you'll discover that heartfelt worship is a wonderful antidote to the stressors of everyday life. So today and every day, worship the Lord with your thoughts, prayers, and actions. Write His name on your heart and rest assured that He, too, has written your name on His.

MORE THOUGHTS ABOUT WORSHIP

*Even the most routine part of your day
can be a spiritual act of worship.*

SARAH YOUNG

*Worship and worry cannot live in the same heart;
they are mutually exclusive.*

RUTH BELL GRAHAM

*Inside the human heart is an undeniable,
spiritual instinct to commune with its Creator.*

JIM CYMBALA

Worship is your spirit responding to God's Spirit.

RICK WARREN

*It is impossible to worship God
and remain unchanged.*

HENRY BLACKABY

*Worship in the truest sense takes place
only when our full attention is on God.*

BILLY GRAHAM

MORE FROM GOD'S WORD

Happy are those who hear the joyful
call to worship, for they will walk
in the light of your presence, Lord.
PSALM 89:15 NLT

All the earth will worship You and sing praise to You.
They will sing praise to Your name.
PSALM 66:4 HCSB

REMEMBER THIS

When you worship God with a sincere heart, He will guide your steps, calm your fears, and bless your life.

GET PRACTICAL

Want to keep things in perspective while you're reducing the stresses of everyday life? Try worshipping God seven days a week, not just on Sunday.

26

DON'T WORRY

What the Bible Says

Therefore do not worry about tomorrow,
for tomorrow will worry about its own things.
Sufficient for the day is its own trouble.

MATTHEW 6:34 NKJV

Because we are imperfect human beings struggling with imperfect circumstances, we worry. Even though we as Christians have the assurance of God's Word, and even though we have the promise of His love and protection, we find ourselves fretting over the inevitable frustrations of everyday life. Jesus understood our concerns when He spoke the reassuring words found in the sixth chapter of Matthew.

Where is the best place to take your worries? Take them to God. Take your troubles to Him; take your fears to Him; take your doubts to Him; take your weaknesses to Him; take your sorrows to Him, and leave them all there. Build your spiritual house upon the Rock that cannot be moved.

Perhaps you are stressed about your future, your health, or your finances. Or perhaps you are simply a worrier by nature. If so, make Matthew 6 a regular part of your daily Bible reading. This beautiful passage will remind you that God still sits in His heaven and you are still His beloved child. Then, perhaps, you will worry a little less and trust God a little more, and that's as it should be because God is trustworthy, and you are protected.

ABOVE AND BEYOND WORRY

The beginning of anxiety is the end of faith, and the beginning of true faith is the end of anxiety.

GEORGE MUELLER

God is bigger than your problems.
Whatever worries press upon you today,
put them in God's hands and leave them there.

BILLY GRAHAM

Today is the tomorrow we worried about yesterday.

DENNIS SWANBERG

Pray, and let God worry.

MARTIN LUTHER

We are not called to be burden-bearers,
but cross-bearers and light-bearers.
We must cast our burdens on the Lord.

CORRIE TEN BOOM

Do not borrow trouble by dreading tomorrow.
It is the dark menace of the future
that makes cowards of us all.

DOROTHY DIX

MORE FROM GOD'S WORD

*Don't worry about anything, but in everything,
through prayer and petition with thanksgiving,
let your requests be made known to God.*

PHILIPPIANS 4:6 HCSB

*Let not your heart be troubled;
you believe in God, believe also in Me.*

JOHN 14:1 NKJV

REMEMBER THIS

Needless worry creates needless stress. So when you're troubled, learn to worry less by trusting God more.

GET PRACTICAL

Using pen and paper, assiduously divide your areas of concern into two categories: the things you can control and the things you can't control. Then resolve never to waste time or energy worrying about the latter. Focus instead on the things you can control and leave the rest up to God.

27

STRESS AND ADDICTION

What the Bible Says

Do not have other gods besides Me.

EXODUS 20:3 HCSB

If you'd like a perfect formula for creating stress, here it is: become addicted to something that destroys your health or sanity.

Ours is a society that glamorizes the use of drugs, alcohol, cigarettes, and other addictive substances. Why? The answer can be summed up in one word: money. Simply put, addictive substances are enormously profitable, so suppliers (of both legal and illegal substances) work overtime to make certain that prospective customers sample—and then become addicted to—their products.

The dictionary defines addiction as "the compulsive need for a habit-forming substance; the condition of being habitually and compulsively occupied with something." That definition is accurate, but incomplete. For Christians, addiction has an additional meaning: it means compulsively worshipping something other than God.

Unless you're living on a deserted island, you know people who are full-blown addicts—If you, or someone you love, is suffering from the blight of addiction, remember this: help is available. Millions of people have overcome addiction and lived to tell about it, so don't give up hope. And if you're one of those fortunate people who hasn't started experimenting with addictive substances, congratulations! You have just have spared yourself a lifetime of headaches and heartaches.

ABOUT ADDICTION

*Some of the most heart-breaking letters
I receive are from people who tell how
alcohol or drugs have ravaged their lives
and destroyed their families.*

BILLY GRAHAM

*Breaking an addiction usually requires
changes in many different areas of life.*

GERALD MAY, M.D.

You have to stop in order to change direction.

ERICH FROMM

*The journey homeward, the process
of homemaking in God, involves
withdrawal from addictive behaviors
that have become normal for us.*

GERALD MAY, MD

*With a strong spiritual foundation,
individuals in recovery are more resilient to stress
and anxiety; they feel more optimistic about life;
and, they experience a sense of belonging
and a renewed sense of purpose.*

DOUGLAS COOK, MD

MORE FROM GOD'S WORD

*Be serious! Be alert! Your adversary the Devil
is prowling around like a roaring lion,
looking for anyone he can devour.*

1 PETER 5:8 HCSB

*Let us walk properly, as in the day,
not in revelry and drunkenness,
not in lewdness and lust, not in strife and envy.*

ROMANS 13:13 NKJV

REMEMBER THIS

Ultimately you and you alone are responsible for controlling your appetites. Others may warn you, help you, or encourage you, but in the end, the habits that rule your life are the very same habits that you yourself have formed. Thankfully, since you formed these habits, you can also break them *if* you decide to do so.

GET PRACTICAL

If a trained mental health professional suggests that you have a problem with eating disorders, alcohol, drugs, or a compulsive behavior, seek treatment immediately. Your future and your life may depend on it.

28

STUDY GOD'S WORD

What the Bible Says

*Your word is a lamp to my feet
and a light to my path.*

PSALM 119:105 NKJV

Another great stress reliever is Bible study. God's Word is unlike any other book. The words of Matthew 4:4 remind us that "man shall not live by bread alone, but by every word that proceedeth out of the mouth of God" (KJV). As Christians, we are instructed to study the Bible and meditate upon its meaning, yet far too many Bibles are laid aside by well-intentioned believers who would like to study the Bible if they "could just find the time."

Warren Wiersbe observed, "When the child of God looks into the Word of God, he sees the Son of God. And he is transformed by the Spirit of God to share in the glory of God." God's Holy Word is, indeed, a life-changing, stress-reducing, one-of-a-kind treasure. And it's up to you to use it that way.

Are you tired? Discouraged? Fearful? Be comforted and trust the promises that God has made to you. Are you worried or stressed? Be confident in God's power. Do you see a difficult future ahead? Be courageous and call upon God. He will protect you and then use you according to His purposes. Are you confused? Listen to the quiet voice of your heavenly Father. He is not a God of confusion. Talk with Him; listen to Him; trust Him, and trust His promises. He is steadfast and He is your Protector—now and forever.

ABOUT BIBLE STUDY

*Study the Bible and observe how the persons
behaved and how God dealt with them.
There is explicit teaching on every condition of life.*

CORRIE TEN BOOM

*The Bible is a Christian's guidebook, and I believe
the knowledge it sheds on pain
and suffering is the great antidote to fear for
suffering people. Knowledge can
dissolve fear as light destroys darkness.*

PHILIP YANCEY

*The Bible is the treasure map that leads us to God's
highest treasure: eternal life.*

MAX LUCADO

*The Bible is a remarkable commentary on
perspective. Through its divine message, we are
brought face to face with issues and tests in daily
living and how, by the power of the Holy Spirit, we
are enabled to respond positively to them.*

LUCI SWINDOLL

*By reading the Scripture I am so renewed that all
nature seems renewed around me and with me.*

THOMAS MERTON

MORE FROM GOD'S WORD

All Scripture is given by inspiration of God, and is profitable for doctrine, for reproof, for correction, for instruction in righteousness.

2 Timothy 3:16 KJV

The counsel of the Lord stands forever, the plans of His heart from generation to generation.

Psalm 33:11 NASB

REMEMBER THIS

Regular Bible study is a powerful tool for maintaining perspective and moderating stress. So turn to the Word every day for guidance, for inspiration, and for Truth with a capital T.

GET PRACTICAL

Read your Bible every morning. No exceptions. When you start each day by studying God's Word, you'll change the quality and direction of your life.

29

UNDERSTANDING AND TREATING MENTAL ILLNESS

What the Bible Says

Why am I so depressed? Why this turmoil within me?
Put your hope in God, for I will still praise Him,
my Savior and my God.

PSALM 42:11 HCSB

They call it mental illness for a very simple reason: it's an illness. Yet all too often, we don't treat it that way. Instead of doing the logical thing, which is seeking professional or medical help, we avoid treatment because we're embarrassed, or uninformed, or afraid, or all of the above.

In almost all cases, mental illness is treatable with medication and counseling. When patients receive initial treatment and then stick to their treatment regimens, they usually get better and stay that way. But left untreated, mental illness presents real dangers to patients' physical health and to their emotional well-being.

If you find yourself feeling "blue" or "manic," perhaps it's a logical reaction to the ups and downs of daily life. But if your feelings of sadness or stress have lasted longer than you think they should—or if someone close to you expresses the opinion that your emotions may have been hijacked by clinical depression, by bipolar disorder, or any other mental illness—it's time to seek professional help without delay.

Some days are light and happy, and some days are not.

We bring light to the dark days of life by turning first to God, and then to family members, to friends, and, when necessary, to medical professionals. When we do, the stress will be relieved, the clouds will eventually part, and the sun will shine once more upon our souls.

—⚬—

ABOUT MENTAL ILLNESS

Every diagnosis is so important because the earlier a mental illness can be detected, diagnosed, and treated, the better off that person can be for the rest of his or her life.

ROSALYNN CARTER

What mental health needs is more sunlight, more candor, more unashamed conversation about illnesses that affect not only individuals, but their families as well.

GLENN CLOSE

We know that mental illness is not something that happens to other people. It touches us all. Why then is mental illness met with so much misunderstanding and fear?

TIPPER GORE

Depression is the inability to construct a future.

ROLLO MAY

Beware of desperate steps; the darkest day,
lived till tomorrow, will have passed away.

WILLIAM COWPER

MORE FROM GOD'S WORD

Let us hold fast the confession of our hope without
wavering, for He who promised is faithful.

HEBREWS 10:23 NASB

This hope we have as an anchor of the soul,
a hope both sure and steadfast.

HEBREWS 6:19 NASB

REMEMBER THIS

If you're feeling discouraged, despondent, or overly stressed, don't hit the panic button and don't keep everything bottled up inside. Talk things over with your spouse, with your physician, and, if necessary, with a counselor you can trust. A second opinion (or a third, fourth, or fifth opinion) is usually helpful. So if your troubles seem overwhelming, it's wise to seek outside help.

GET PRACTICAL

If you or someone you know seems to be dangerously sad or manic don't sit around and wait for things to get better. Seek professional help ASAP.

30

MANAGE MONEY WISELY

What the Bible Says

*Good planning and hard work lead to prosperity,
but hasty shortcuts lead to poverty.*

PROVERBS 21:5 NLT

If you're plagued by stress-inducing financial troubles, you're not alone. You inhabit a world where financial stress is rampant. How can you resolve the stress of managing money wisely? Oftentimes, it's simply a matter of spending less.

Living on a budget sounds so easy, but it can be so hard. After all, we live in a world that is filled to the brim with wonderful things to buy and wonderful people telling us that we need to buy those things. But sometimes our desires for more and better stuff can overload our ability to pay for the things we want. That's when Old Man Trouble arrives at the door.

The answer to the problem of overspending is straight forward. What's required is discipline. First, we must earn money through honest work for which we are well-suited; then, we must spend less than we earn (and save the rest intelligently). This strategy of earning and saving money is simple to understand but much harder to put into practice. Thankfully, God gives us clear instructions that, when followed, can lead us on the proper path.

God's Word reminds us again and again that our Creator expects us to lead disciplined lives. And when we pause to consider how much work needs to be done, we realize that self-discipline is not simply a proven way to get ahead, it's also an integral part of God's plan for our lives. If we genuinely seek to be faithful stewards of our time, our talents, and our resources, we must adopt a disciplined approach to life. There's simply no other way.

ABOUT MANAGING MONEY

Here's a recipe for handling money wisely: take a heaping helping of common sense, add a sizeable portion of self-discipline, and mix with prayer.
MARIE T. FREEMAN

Discipline understands that the best way to get rich quick is to get rich slow.
DAVE RAMSEY

If you work hard and maintain an attitude of gratitude, you'll find it easier to manage your finances every day.
JOHN MAXWELL

You cannot bring about prosperity by discouraging thrift.
WILLIAM BOETCKER

Industry, perseverance, and frugality make fortune yield.
BEN FRANKLIN

MORE FROM GOD'S WORD

Keep your lives free from the love of money,
and be satisfied with what you have.

HEBREWS 13:5 NCV

A faithful man will abound with blessings, but he
who makes haste to be rich will not go unpunished.

PROVERBS 28:20 NASB

REMEMBER THIS

Money problems, when allowed to multiply, can create massive amounts of stress. Overspending creates stress; financial discipline reduces it. So if you really want to reduce stress, you may first need to reduce your spending.

GET PRACTICAL

If you're facing a financial crisis, don't face it alone. Enlist God's help. And then, when you've finished praying about your problem, don't be afraid to seek help from financial counselors, from mentors, or from knowledgeable family members or friends.

31
SEEK GOD'S GUIDANCE

WHAT THE BIBLE SAYS

Trust in the Lord with all your heart,
and lean not on your own understanding;
in all your ways acknowledge Him,
and He shall direct your paths.
PROVERBS 3:5–6 NKJV

When we trust Him with all our hearts, our heavenly Father carefully guides us over the peaks and valleys of life. Whether we find ourselves at the pinnacle of the mountain or the darkest depths of the valley, the loving heart of God is always there with us.

As Christians, we have every reason to live joyously and courageously. After all, Christ has already fought and won our battle for us—He did so on the cross at Calvary. But despite Christ's sacrifice, and despite God's promises, we may become confused or disoriented by the endless complications and countless distractions of life here in the twenty-first century.

C. S. Lewis observed, "I don't doubt that the Holy Spirit guides your decisions from within when you make them with the intention of pleasing God. The error would be to think that He speaks only within, whereas in reality He speaks also through Scripture, the Church, Christian friends, and books." These words remind us that God has many ways to make Himself known. Our challenge is to make ourselves open to His instruction.

So, if you're unsure of your next step, lean upon God's promises and lift your prayers to Him. Remember that God is always near—always trying to get His message through. Open yourself to Him every day, and trust Him to guide your path. When you do, you'll be protected today, tomorrow, and forever.

ABOUT GOD'S GUIDANCE

*God will prove to you how good
and acceptable and perfect
His will is when He's got His hands
on the steering wheel of your life.*

STUART AND JILL BRISCOE

*God never leads us astray.
He knows exactly
where He's taking us.
Our job is to obey.*

CHARLES SWINDOLL

*Get into the habit of dealing
with God about everything.*

OSWALD CHAMBERS

*Don't bother to give God instructions;
just report for duty.*

CORRIE TEN BOOM

MORE FROM GOD'S WORD

The LORD says, "I will guide you along
the best pathway for your life.
I will advise you and watch over you."
PSALM 32:8 NLT

Show me thy ways, O LORD;
teach me thy paths. Lead me in thy truth,
and teach me: for thou art the God
of my salvation; on thee do I wait all the day.
PSALM 25:4–5 KJV

—⚬⚬⚬—

REMEMBER THIS

If you make plans that are outside of God's will, you will experience unwelcome consequences. A far better strategy is to consult God earnestly and consistently before you embark upon the next stage of your life's journey. As you sense His intentions, follow them.

GET PRACTICAL

If you sincerely want to reduce stress, pray for God's guidance and ask for His help. When you ask, He will answer.

32

THE WISDOM OF MODERATION

What the Bible Says

Moderation is better than muscle,
self-control better than political power.

PROVERBS 16:32 MSG

Moderation and wisdom are traveling companions. If we are wise, we must learn to temper our appetites, our desires, and our impulses. When we do, we are blessed, in part, because God has created a world in which temperance is rewarded and intemperance is inevitably punished.

When we allow our appetites to run wild, they usually do. When we abandon moderation, we forfeit the inner peace that God offers—but does not guarantee—to His children. When we live intemperate lives, we rob ourselves of countless blessings that would have otherwise been ours.

God's instructions are clear: If we seek to live wisely, we must be moderate in our appetites and disciplined in our behavior. To do otherwise is an affront to Him *and* to ourselves.

Moderation is especially difficult in a society such as ours, but the rewards of moderation are numerous and long lasting. No one can force you to control your appetites. The decision to live temperately (and wisely) is yours and yours alone. And so are the consequences.

THE SIMPLE LIFE

Want to reduce stress? Here's a simple solution: Simplify your life. Unfortunately, it's a solution that's easier said than done. After all, you live in a world where simplicity is in short supply.

Think for a moment about the complexity of your everyday life and compare it to the lives of your ancestors. Certainly, you are the beneficiary of many technological innovations, but those innovations have come at a price: in all likelihood, your world is highly complex. Unless you take firm control of your time and your life, you may be overwhelmed by a stress-inducing tidal wave of complexity that threatens your happiness.

Your heavenly Father understands the joy of living simply, and so should you. So do yourself a favor: keep your life as simple as possible. Simplicity is, indeed, genius. By simplifying your life, you are destined to improve it.

—⁓—

CONSIDER THIS

God's Word instructs you to be moderate and disciplined as you guard your body, your mind, and your heart. So when in doubt, be a little more moderate than necessary.

THE REWARDS OF MODERATION

Virtue—even attempted virtue—brings light;
indulgence brings fog.

C. S. LEWIS

A society that pursues pleasure runs the risk of
raising expectations ever higher, so that true
contentment always lies tantalizingly out of reach.

PHILIP YANCEY AND PAUL BRAND

To many, total abstinence
is easier than perfect moderation.

ST. AUGUSTINE

There is absolutely no evidence that complexity
and materialism lead to happiness. On the
contrary, there is plenty of evidence that simplicity
and spirituality lead to joy, a blessedness
that is better than happiness.

DENNIS SWANBERG

Better is a little with content
than much with contention.

BEN FRANKLIN

As faithful stewards of what we have, ought we not
to give earnest thought to our staggering surplus?

ELISABETH ELLIOT

MORE FROM GOD'S WORD

Do what is right and good in the Lord's sight,
so that you may prosper and so that you may
enter and possess the good land the Lord
your God swore to give your fathers.
DEUTERONOMY 6:18 HCSB

Discipline yourself for the purpose of godliness.
1 TIMOTHY 4:7 NASB

REMEMBER THIS

Perhaps you think that the more stuff you acquire, the happier you'll be. If so, think again. Too much stuff means too much stress, so start simplifying now.

GET PRACTICAL

Overindulgence creates stress; moderation reduces it. The choice to be moderate—a choice, by the way, that you must make day by day and moment by moment—is up to you.

33

GOD CAN HANDLE IT

What the Bible Says

I will lift up my eyes to the hills—
from whence comes my help?
My help comes from the LORD,
who made heaven and earth.

PSALM 121:1–2 NKJV

Stressful days are an inevitable fact of modern life. So how do we best cope with the challenges of our demanding, twenty-first-century world? By turning our days and our lives over to God. Elisabeth Elliot writes, "If my life is surrendered to God, all is well. Let me not grab it back, as though it were in peril in His hand but would be safer in mine!" Yet even the most devoted Christian may, at times, seek to grab the reins and proclaim, "I'm in charge!" To do so is foolish, prideful, and stressful.

When we seek to impose our own wills upon the world, we invite needless stress into our lives. But, when we turn our lives and our hearts over to God—when we accept His will instead of vainly seeking to impose our own—we discover the inner peace that can be ours through Him.

Do you feel overwhelmed by the stresses of daily life? Turn your concerns and your prayers over to God. Trust Him. Trust Him completely. Trust Him today. Trust Him always. When it comes to the inevitable challenges of this day, hand them over to the Lord completely and without reservation. He knows your needs and will meet those needs in His own way and in His own time if you let Him.

RELY UPON HIM

God is a never-ending source of support and courage for those of us who call upon Him. When we are weary, He gives us strength. When we see no hope, God reminds us of His promises. When we grieve, God wipes away our tears.

God will hold your hand and walk with you every day of your life if you let Him. So even if your circumstances are difficult, trust the Father. His love is eternal and His goodness endures forever.

CONSIDER THIS

God can handle your problems. All of them. No problem is too big for Him . . . not even yours.

GOD IS BIGGER
THAN EVERY PROBLEM YOU FACE

*Often God has to shut a door in our face
so that He can subsequently open the door
through which He wants us to go.*

CATHERINE MARSHALL

*The next time you're disappointed, don't panic.
Don't give up. Just be patient and let God
remind you He's still in control.*

MAX LUCADO

*He can accomplish anything He chooses to do.
If He ever asks you to do something,
He Himself will enable you to do it.*

HENRY BLACKABY

*God is, must be, our answer to every question
and every cry of need.*

HANNAH WHITALL SMITH

*You may not know what you
are going to do; you only know
that God knows what He is going to do.*

OSWALD CHAMBERS

*The presence of hope in the invincible
sovereignty of God drives out fear.*

JOHN PIPER

MORE FROM GOD'S WORD

His divine power has given us everything we need
for a godly life through our knowledge of him who
called us by his own glory and goodness.

2 Peter 1:3 NIV

Great is thy faithfulness.

Lamentations 3:23 KJV

REMEMBER THIS

God is big enough and strong enough to solve any challenge you will ever face. When every other support system fails, you can still rely on Him.

GET PRACTICAL

Today, think about ways that you can tap into God's strength. For starters, try prayer, worship, and praise.

34

ENTRUST YOUR FUTURE TO GOD

What the Bible Says

For I know the thoughts that I think toward you, says the LORD, thoughts of peace and not of evil, to give you a future and a hope. Then you will call upon Me and go and pray to Me, and I will listen to you.

JEREMIAH 29:11–12 NKJV

Because of the promises we find in God's Word, we can have hope for the future, no matter how troublesome our present circumstances may seem. After all, God has promised that we are His throughout eternity. He has told us that we must place our hope in Him.

We all face disappointments and failures while we're here on earth, but those are only temporary defeats. Of course, this world can be a place of stresses, trials, and tribulations, but when we place our trust in the Giver of all things good, we are secure. God has promised us peace, joy, and eternal life. And He keeps His promises today, tomorrow, and forever.

Are you willing to place your future in the hands of a loving and all-knowing God? Do you trust in the ultimate goodness of His plan for your life? Will you face today's challenges with optimism and hope? You should. After all, God created you for a very important purpose: His purpose. And you still have important work to do: His work.

Today, as you live in the present and look to the future, remember that God has a plan for you. Act and believe accordingly.

—✺—

DISCOVERING GOD'S PLANS

Do you want to experience a life filled with abundance and peace? If so, here's a word of warning: you'll need to resist the temptation to do things your way and commit, instead, to do things God's way.

God has plans for your life. Big plans. But He won't force you to follow His will; to the contrary, He has given you free will, the ability to make decisions on your own. With the freedom to choose comes the responsibility of living with the consequences of the choices you make.

The most important decision of your life is, of course, your commitment to accept Jesus Christ as your personal Lord and Savior. And once your eternal destiny is secured, you will undoubtedly ask yourself the question "What now, Lord?" If you earnestly seek God's will for your life, you will find it in time.

Sometimes God's plans are crystal clear, but other times, He leads you through the wilderness before He delivers you to the promised land. So be patient, keep searching, and keep praying. When you do, God will answer your prayers and make His plans known.

God is right here, and He intends to use you in wonderful, unexpected ways. You'll discover those plans by doing things His way, and you'll be eternally grateful that you did.

CONSIDER THIS

With God as your partner, your future is bright. So it's wise to focus your thoughts and energy on future opportunities rather than on past disappointments.

THOUGHTS ABOUT YOUR FUTURE

The future lies all before us. Shall it only be a slight advance upon what we usually do? Ought it not to be a bound, a leap forward to altitudes of endeavor and success undreamed of before?

ANNIE ARMSTRONG

Hoping for a good future without investing in today is like a farmer waiting for a crop without ever planting any seed.

JOHN MAXWELL

Don't ever forget there are more firsts to come.

DENNIS SWANBERG

That we may not complain of what is, let us see God's hand in all events; and, that we may not be afraid of what shall be, let us see all events in God's hand.

MATTHEW HENRY

*Take courage. We walk in the wilderness
today and in the Promised Land tomorrow.*

D. L. MOODY

MORE FROM GOD'S WORD

*There is surely a future hope for you,
and your hope will not be cut off.*

PROVERBS 23:18 NIV

*But if we look forward to something we don't have
yet, we must wait patiently and confidently.*

ROMANS 8:25 NLT

REMEMBER THIS

With God as your partner, you can overcome any obstacle. When you place your future in His hands, you have absolutely nothing to fear.

GET PRACTICAL

God has a wonderful plan for your life. The time to start looking for that plan and living it is now.

ESSENTIAL TIME-MANAGEMENT TIPS THAT CAN SAVE YOU HUNDREDS OF HOURS EACH YEAR

Start your day with God. Start every morning by spending time with your Creator. Decide how much of your time He deserves, and then give it to Him. He will help you keep things in perspective as you prioritize your day and organize your life.

Know your goals. When you have a clear understanding of your long-term, medium-term, and short-term goals, you'll be better equipped to plan your day, your week, and your year. Make sure your goals are in writing and refer to them often.

Begin the day with a prioritized to-do list. Don't just compose a long list of things that need to be done. Prioritize the things on your list. Then, as you tackle the jobs on your list, make certain that A-priority items come first.

Also have a to-don't list. Many low-priority tasks don't belong on your to-do list. The dictionary defines the word busywork as "work that keeps a person busy but has little value in itself." This is the sort of work you should assiduously avoid.

Don't postpone unpleasant high-priority tasks. You may be tempted to put off unpleasant tasks until the end of the day, or for that matter, the end of the week. To do so is tempting, but it's contrary to your best interests. A far better strategy is to get the unpleasant work out of the way as soon as possible. When you do, you'll enjoy the rest of the day, and you'll be more productive too.

Identify and vanquish your personal time thieves. Here in the twenty-first century, we're confronted with a near-endless array of time-squandering activities: Twitter, Facebook, Instagram, other forms of social media, and all those apps on your phone, *plus* hundreds of TV channels and movie sites. Either you will summon the self-discipline to control these time bandits, or they will most certainly control you.

Learn to say no early and often. The best way to handle some time-gobbling commitments is to avoid them in the first place. Since you can't do everything, you must learn to say no politely, forcefully, and as often as necessary. And while you're at it, remember that if you don't prioritize your day, other people will most certainly do the job for you.

Don't become a slave to your smartphone. Just because you have the ability to check your texts, e-mails, and social media accounts minute by minute doesn't mean that you should.

When performing high-priority tasks, turn off your phone. When you're engaged in high-priority tasks, don't let your phone get in the way; all calls should be put on hold.

Stay organized. Get into the habit of spending a few minutes every day organizing your workspace, putting emails into folders, being sure that your devices are backed up, and generally doing whatever you can to fight disorder and entropy. Order saves time; chaos squanders it.

Be sure to get enough rest. If you're constantly sleep deprived, you'll make needless mistakes that will require time and energy to fix. God wants you to get enough rest. The world wants you to burn the candle at both ends. Trust God.

Refuse to worry about the things you cannot control. Worry consumes two precious commodities: time and energy. So instead of wasting your emotional resources on matters you cannot control, turn them over to God. Focus instead on the things that you can change and leave the rest up to Him.

YES, YOU CAN LEARN
TO MANAGE STRESS AND
TAKE CONTROL OF YOUR LIFE

Jesus said to him, "If you can believe,
all things are possible to him who believes."

MARK 9:23 NKJV

Are you secretly afraid that you simply don't have what it takes to manage stress and take control of your life? If so, please remember this: with God, all things are possible.

God has put you in a particular place, at a specific time of His choosing. He has an assignment that is uniquely yours. And whether you know it or not, He's equipped you with everything you need to fulfill His purpose and achieve His plans. You can accomplish those plans with greater efficiency and less stress if you apply the principles in this book and, more importantly, if you enlist God as your partner in every endeavor. The Lord can help you do things you never dreamed possible. Your job is to let Him.

———∞———

ABOUT THE AUTHOR

Criswell Freeman is a Doctor of Clinical Psychology who, over the last twenty-five years, has authored numerous Christian, inspirational, and self-help titles. With over 20 million books in print, he usually avoids publicity and prefers to work quietly—and often anonymously—from his home in Nashville, Tennessee.